Beyond SUBJECT MATTER EXPERTISE

Strategies for Instructing Adults

GLENN ROSS JOHNSON
and ROBERT MAGNAN

Atwood Publishing
Madison, Wisconsin

Beyond Subject Matter Expertise: Strategies for Instructing Adults
By Glenn Ross Johnson and Robert Magnan

Cover design by TLC Graphics, www.tlcgraphics.com

TABLE OF CONTENTS

PREFACE

Maybe you've just been given the opportunity to teach or train adults — perhaps at a college, perhaps through your business or another organization. If so, congratulations!

Maybe you've been teaching or training adults and you want to be able to teach or train more effectively, prepare more efficiently, or both. That's great!

Whatever your situation, if you're a subject matter expert who's new to instructing adults, this book is for you.

You can't necessarily train or teach effectively just because you know a lot about the subject. Your skills and knowledge are important, of course, but you must be able to help others develop those skills and acquire that knowledge. As the title states, you must go *beyond subject matter expertise*.

This book is intended to help you a lot in just a little time. It's structured around some basic questions that you should be asking and answering as you begin preparing to train or to teach. Some of the questions consist of a series of questions; some of the answers may lead to other questions. You can choose your own path through the book according to your needs and interests.

For the sake of simplicity, we'll use generic terms — instructor (whether training or teaching), "learner," "course," and "session."

Beyond Subject Matter Expertise: Strategies for Instructing Adults is an outgrowth of many years of research and experience in teaching adults in diverse settings: conducting seminars for medical doctors; giving presentations to adult groups during conferences and conventions; serving with the Instructor Group of the 3rd Armored Division U.S. Army; teaching undergraduate and graduate students enrolled at the college level; and implementing and directing a Center for Teaching Excellence for faculty members and teaching assistants at the university level.

My four adult children (ages mid- to late 40s) have been involved in teaching adults and all four have interacted with me about their experiences in teaching adults. My oldest daughter, Carrie, is a programmer for a major computer company, and she is called on to make presentations to other adults who need instruction with new programs. My oldest son, Ross, works for a large accounting firm, and he is called on to teach others in accounting matters. My youngest son, Martin, works for a precision tool company, and he makes presentations involving marketing strategies. My youngest daughter, Julie, is a math teacher in a public school, and there are times when she instructs teachers new to the school system.

I've compiled here the basics for instructing adults. It provides an array of instructional strategies, a way to systematically engage adults in the learning process, and suggestions for improving verbal interactions between instructor and learners.

— Glenn Ross Johnson

Linda Babler, president of Atwood Publishing, invited me to work on this project as an editor, to benefit from my experience in teaching at the postsecondary level and in editing and writing books in education and business. Glenn then invited me to contribute more substantively, as co-author.

I enjoyed working on this book. However, that's not what's important, not to you. What's important to you is what you can learn from this book so you can teach or train more effectively. So, let's start!

— Robert Magnan

UNDERSTAND YOUR SITUATION!

If you've never trained or taught, you probably have a lot of questions. But whatever your experience, you should be asking and answering the following questions. (This book will help you answer some of them.)

- What's the subject matter?
    - How specifically has it been demarcated for you by the powers that be?
- Who are the learners?
    - What do they know already about the subject matter?
    - What skills do they have already in the subject area?
    - Why are they in this course?
    - What motivates them to learn?
- What are the purposes of this course? Why is it being offered?
- What are the gaps that should be your focus? In other words, what do the learners need to get from where they are to where the organization wants them to be?
- What are your expectations for the learners? (We'll help you with this question in the next section, "Set Behavioral Objectives.")
- What are your resources and your constraints?

- What's available? What materials? What facilities? What equipment? How much time? How much money?

- What rules are you expected to follow as an instructor?

  - Are you doing this course in your own organization? If so, you're probably familiar with the rules and the cultural norms — and there may not be many formal expectations. Know what's expected of you as instructor.

  - Are you doing this course at an educational institution? If so, there are policies, regulations, and administrative requirements, as well as cultural norms. Find out the rules.

- What's the best way to help these learners fill the gaps you've identified? (We'll help you with this question in the next four sections, "Develop a Schedule," "Know the Learners," "Select the Strategies," and "Select the Materials.")

SET BEHAVIORAL OBJECTIVES

Your course should have a goal or goals. A course goal is a broad statement about the outcomes that are expected, in terms of the knowledge and/or skills that the learners will acquire.

Goals show the big picture. From goals we create learning objectives.

These objectives state more specifically what the learners are expected to achieve as a result of instruction. The purpose of objectives is to ensure that instruction is focused clearly enough that both learners and instructor know what results are expected and, if those results are to be assessed, to enable the instructor to measure them objectively.

How will you be able to know whether or not the learners have achieved the expected outcomes? You specify the objectives in terms of behavior — what you want them to do. These are *behavioral* objectives.

Use Action Verbs

Word behavioral objectives with verbs such as the following:

- demonstrate
- analyze
- show
- express
- evaluate
- build
- organize
- create
- develop

- write
- plan
- apply
- make

Avoid using verbs that make objectives difficult to measure, such as the following:

- know
- comprehend
- understand
- appreciate
- enjoy
- become familiar with
- study
- know
- be aware
- become acquainted with
- perceive
- gain knowledge of
- cover
- learn
- realize

Let's try an example.

Imagine that you're the resident spreadsheet guru. The boss just said, "None of the people in marketing know how to use Excel! Give them some training on spreadsheet basics!"

So, now you're instructor with only an informal and vague statement of purpose. You have to get specifics from the boss or otherwise determine what she meant by "use Excel" and "spreadsheet basics."

Once you've figured out what you're expected to cover in your course, you can then create a course objective. You might write something like this: "By the end of this course, learners will be able to use Excel to create a spreadsheet, enter and edit labels and values and formulas, save and update workbooks, to modify and copy data, …" and so on.

Now, what knowledge and skills would the learners need in order to do those things with Excel? You break each of those areas of use into actions. (That can be difficult for a subject matter expert who uses Excel almost instinctively.)

Then, you frame those actions in terms of objectives involving *showing* abilities — behavioral objectives.

Take One Step

This is the first step to writing a behavioral objective — and maybe the only one you'll need. Take your purpose — what you want the learners to know, understand, and/or be able to do at the end — and convert it into behavioral objectives. *How will you know that they have the knowledge, understanding, or ability?*

That step is simple to understand and relatively simple in practice — if you use good verbs, verbs that describe behaviors, such as those in the first list above, and avoid verbs that refer to mental and emotional states, such as those in the second list.

The key in creating behavioral objectives is to *specify in observable behaviors*. Here are two objectives:

- Learners will know how to create a spreadsheet.

- Learners will be able to enter labels, values, and formulas.

How can you be sure that they "know" and "are able"? And how can the learners be sure? After all, we sometimes believe we know something or can do something — and then find out we don't or we can't.

So, we must phrase objectives in terms of behavior:

- Learners will create a spreadsheet.

- Learners will enter labels, values, and formulas.

Maybe those objectives are specific enough for your purposes. Maybe you would understand, the learners would understand, and if they learned how to do those things, the boss would be satisfied.

If you have no reason to make your objectives more specific, feel free to skip to the next section. Otherwise, read on.

Take a Second Step

But maybe those objectives are still not specific enough. Maybe your boss wants you to be able to use them to evaluate the learners at the end of the course. Then, to make your objectives even more specific, you take the next step: specify. *How can you phrase what you want explicitly enough so that learners understand what is expected of them?* If you're responsible for assessing their progress in terms of a grade, add to that question, *and so anybody could evaluate them appropriately?*

This step can be difficult. Most instructors tend to state objectives in such broad terms that it's difficult for learners to interpret them into specifics — and difficult to use them to evaluate the learners.

For this step, we need two basic specifics:

- Conditions

- Criteria for performance

Consider this objective: "On an asphalt track, the individual will run the 100-meter dash in less than 17 seconds."

We know the conditions ("on an asphalt track"), the type of measurable behavior ("run the 100-meter dash"), and the acceptable performance level ("less than 17 seconds"). This is an example of a specific behavioral objective. Without the specified acceptable performance level, almost anyone could achieve the objective — although it might take 25 seconds. 30 seconds, 45 seconds, one minute ....

If we were intending to give grades, we could specify several performance levels: "On an asphalt track, the individual will run the 100-meter dash in less than 15 seconds for an A, in less than 16 seconds for a B, in less than 17 seconds for a C, and in less than 18 seconds for a D.".

Beware of words like "correctly" and "successfully" as performance standards. What do they mean? In some cases, it may be obvious. In many cases, though, it's not. Specify.

So now we make those two Excel objectives more specific:

- On a company computer, using Excel without access to any guidelines or other assistance ...
  - learners will create a spreadsheet consisting of 7 columns and 12 rows, within 10 seconds.
  - learners will take a list of 7 labels, 84 values, and 7 formulas and enter those labels, values, and formulas in that spreadsheet with at least 97% accuracy, within eight minutes.

Obviously, very specific objectives take a lot of time and effort and a list of them might overwhelm the learners. Make only as many objectives as you need for your purposes and make them only as specific as necessary.

Test Your Objectives

How do you know when you've got a good behavioral objective? Test it with role-playing. Ask a friend to play the instructor and read the objective. Then you play the learner and ask your friend the instructor to give you a grade. The results should show how well you've specified the behavior you want.

If you're responsible for evaluating and grading the learners, you've now got the basics for doing so. If you don't have that responsibility, you've got something to give the learners so they can evaluate themselves — and a way for you to evaluate how effectively you've done your job.

Focus on your objectives as you plan the course, as you choose strategies and tactics and materials, as you prepare for each session, and as you evaluate the learners.

(For more, check "More about Setting Behavioral Objectives" at the end of this book.)

DEVELOP A SCHEDULE

To get the learners from where they are to where they need to be, you need a map that sequences the steps in time — a schedule (aka syllabus, program, or agenda).

That map may already have been outlined, perhaps in some detail, either by the powers that be or *de facto* by an assigned textbook or manual. If you've been given a detailed schedule, you may be ready to move on to the next section. If you've been given a book, you may have a choice: you can either *follow* the book, which may not be quite right for your situation and may not target the objectives you've set, or you can *use* the book — as a resource but not as a guide. If the book is determining the steps you take, you will still need to develop them into a schedule. (By the way, if you use a book, make sure that the copies will be available in time and in sufficient supply.)

If you choose to create a schedule your way, congratulations! Read on.

One of the problems that subject matter experts encounter when training or teaching is that they know their material so well that they may not feel a need to draw up any schedule for the course or any plans for individual sessions. However, it's unwise to improvise and unfair for the learners.

To make a course schedule, you start by sketching out a map: figure out a logical progression for covering all of what the learners need in order to achieve the objectives. First, determine the steps, in order. Second, allot those steps to the sessions of the course, according to the amount of time you expect each step to take. Third, once you have a list of the sessions and the steps for each, you're ready to move on.

We advise putting your schedule on a handout for the learners. This is a good idea if you're working in a business setting; it may be required if you're in an academic environment.

As a heading, put your name and any contact information you wish to provide: e.g., phone number(s) and e-mail address. In addition to the schedule, you may wish to include your course objectives and any rules and expectations. Make it easy for the learners to read and refer to the handout.

KNOW ABOUT ADULT LEARNERS

No, you can't know the individual learners before you begin the course, at least not in terms of how they learn. But you can start with some generalizations that will help you plan. Two key factors are adult learning principles and learning styles.

Principles of Adult Learning

Here are five basic principles of adult learning to keep in mind as you consider strategies, tactics, and materials. These are nothing new to you; what may be new is applying these principles to training or teaching, to working with the learners in your course.

Adult learners are practical. They want skills and knowledge that can improve the quality of their work and personal lives. They want learning to be relevant to their needs, interests, activities, goals, and problems. They want reasons for learning. How can they apply what they're learning?

- Tell them explicitly how the things they're learning will be useful to them in their work.

- Draw upon their experience and knowledge whenever it's relevant to the topic at hand.

- Relate theories and concepts to their experiences and situations.

Adult learners are goal-oriented. When they enroll in a course, they usually know what goal they want to attain. Learners appreciate an educational program that is aimed at their goals and organized appropriately.

- Give them the course objectives as you begin the course.

- Make sure that each session and all your activities are aimed at the course objectives.

Adult learners differ widely by their knowledge and their life and work experience.

- Don't expect any one approach, strategy, or example to work for all the learners in your course.

Adult learners need to be autonomous, free to direct themselves.

- Involve them actively in the learning process.

- Work with their perspectives to the extent practical.

- Allow them to work on projects that fit their needs and interests.

- Give them opportunities to work in groups and to assume responsibility for presentations.

Adult learners demand respect.

- Acknowledge the value of their experience and knowledge.

- Treat them as your peers.

- Allow them to express their opinions freely.

We close this brief section on the characteristics of adult learners with a caution. In an overview of adult learning for the *International Encyclopedia of Education*, Stephen Brookfield made the following comment that you should always keep in mind:

Generalizations about "the adult learner," "adults as learners," or "the nature of adult learning" imply that people over 25 form a homogenous entity simply by virtue of their chronological age. Yet the differences of class, culture, ethnicity, personality, cognitive style, learning patterns, life experiences, and gender among adults are far more significant than the fact that they are not children or adolescents.

Learning Styles

People learn in different ways. That's obvious. Beyond that, it gets complicated — too complicated to cover here. So, we'll go with quick and practical.

One basic approach to understanding how we process information is in terms of *sensory dominance*: visual, auditory, and tactile/kinesthetic.

- *Visual* learners learn through seeing. They learn best through visual displays, such as illustrations, charts, diagrams, flip charts, transparencies, and videos.

- *Auditory* learners learn through listening. They learn best through lectures and discussions.

- *Tactile or kinesthetic* learners learn through touching and doing. They learn best through a hands-on approach, through exposure to real things and real experiences.

The key words here are *sensory* and *dominance*. We can all learn through our eyes, our ears, and our touch. A learning style is a question of which way dominates, which is most natural.

Some researchers and many educators have questioned whether styles make a difference in learning. However, it seems undeniable that people learn in different ways. The bottom line for you as an instructor is that you'll be more effective if you vary your methods and materials as much as possible.

For example, if you do a presentation, you should not just talk; you should also display the important points, using words and illustrations, and, if possible, involve the learners physically. It's natural to use whatever methods fit your own learning style. However, what works for you doesn't work for all the people in your class.

If you lecture, you may use thousands of words. That may be good for auditory learners, but for visual learners, "A picture is worth a thousand words," and for tactile/kinesthetic learners, "Touching and doing is worth a thousand pictures." Variety is the key.

SELECT THE STRATEGIES

The following five major interacting variables will determine to a great extent how effectively you will train or teach adults:

- your personal characteristics: e.g., personality, knowledge, skills, and experiences

- the characteristics of learners: knowledge and skills, personality, and attitude toward the subject, the course, and you

- the way you structure the course

- the learning environment: e.g., layout, furniture, lighting, size of the room, size of the class

- the instructional strategies you choose

It seems that the strategies are the most important variable.

There are three general types of strategies:

- "instructor talks, shows, or does" — presentations (e.g., lectures, demonstrations, etc.)

- "instructor and students talk" — questions and answers, discussions

- "learners do" — experiential activities

There are also cooperative activities, in which learners work together in groups. In addition, learners may also individually give presentations: "learner talks, shows, or does."

Focus on Your Objectives

How do you determine which strategies to use? The choice depends primarily on the subject matter and your objectives. It also depends on the learners — what they already know and their learning styles — and the need for variety. Finally, it's naturally influenced by your personality and learning style.

- If your objectives involve knowing a lot of factual information, presentations may be appropriate.

- If your objectives involve affective behavior (values, attitudes), role-playing and simulation may be more effective than presentations.

- If your objectives involve using tools (psychomotor skills), provide hands-on opportunities — experiential activities.

- If your objectives involve group dynamics, consider cooperative activities.

- If your objectives involve applying what the learners know, consider asking questions and discussion.

If there are two or more strategies that would be appropriate, how do you choose?

Maybe you don't need to choose. In fact, maybe using two or more strategies would be best.

But if you need or want to choose a single strategy, consider what you know about the learners and what information you expect them to acquire, recall, and use. How familiar should they be with the subject matter? How comfortable are they likely to be with each other?

Next, consider what each of your strategy choices would require. What materials or equipment? Audiotapes, slides, computers, simulation or other programs, films, etc.? What facilities? Another location? Other people, such as a guest subject matter expert? How much of your time to prepare and make arrangements?

If any consideration supersedes all others, it would be how the learners learn best. You're training or teaching so that the learners acquire knowledge and/or develop skills. As obvious as this point might seem, many instructors believe otherwise: "I just provide the content matter; it's up to them to learn" — as if teaching or training could happen without learning. "I trained/taught successfully, although the learners all failed to learn."

Find Out What They Know Already

What do the learners know already? And how well do they know it? How well can they use what they know? You may not have more than assumptions and guesses before the first session. But then, you can find out.

Toward the end of a session, you can test their knowledge of the material to be covered in the following session. You can ask questions that they answer orally or in writing or even (for true-or-false, yes-or-no questions) with a show of hands. (The questions you use could be questions you intend to use in testing the learners later.)

Vary Your Strategies

You should vary your instructional strategies and your materials for the greater benefit of the learners. Remember that their learning styles differ and their experiences are quite varied.

Many subject matter experts tend to use primarily or only presentations. That may be easier for them, but it's not always or even usually better for the learners. It should not be all "instructor talks, shows, or does." It may be more effective to also use "instructor and students talk," "learners do," and even "learner talks, shows, or does."

So, here are the basics of the following types of methods:

- Presentation ("instructor talks")

- Discussion ("instructor and students talk together")

- Cooperative Activities ("learners work in groups")

- Experiential Activities ("learners do")

Presentation

This strategy has some important advantages. It can be good for providing information and highlighting the most important facts and the major points. It's time-efficient. (This is especially true if you can use your notes and materials more than once.) It can provide more structure and organization, which can make it easier for the learners to understand — or at least to take notes.

There are also considerable disadvantages. Presentations can be boring, especially when the instructor simply reads his or her notes. This is even worse if it's done in a monotone or a voice that's otherwise irritating. Presentations do not actively involve the learners, particularly if they're busy trying to take notes. There's some truth in the comment that "a lecture is the quickest way to get the notes of an instructor into the notes of a student, without passing through the mind of either."

If you do a presentation, keep it under 12-15 minutes. If it must be longer, break it into sections, with pauses for questions, discussion, or some application of the information presented.

People listening to a presentation tend to remember what they hear first and last. Keep this in mind when you plan a presentation — start strong and finish strong, summarizing your main points and emphasizing their importance.

Be as concrete as possible. Use images and analogies. Give examples. Provide facts, of course, but don't bury the learners in information; make sure they understand why the facts should matter to them.

Ask Questions

If you choose to do presentations, you can at least involve the learners by pausing every few minutes to ask questions about the material you've presented. There are various ways to use questions.

You can start with questions that elicit short answers, a few words. Depending on the subject matter, it may be possible to break the students into small groups to discuss, for example, real-world uses of the material.

When you outline your presentation, you can think about good questions to ask and issues of sequence and timing and then write down the questions. It usually works better to direct questions to the group in general, instead of singling out individuals. If a learner mumbles an answer or phrases it poorly, repeat it so that all can hear and rephrase it so all can understand.

You may also want to develop a question to ask to start your presentation and then repeat the question near the end of the session: "Recall the question I raised at the beginning of this session." Ask learners to provide answers.

If things are not going as well as you'd expected, you can try asking some very basic questions, such as these:

- How could you use what we've been covering?

- Could you give me an example of this?

When in trouble, connect with their experiences.

By the way, if you intend to make your presentations interactive, as we encourage you to do, you should start early in the course, perhaps with your first presentation. Let the learners know from the start that you expect them to participate. How? By asking questions during your first presentation.

Finally, something that we can't stress enough — give them time to answer. It takes the average adult learner longer to think of an answer to the average question than it takes the average trainer or teacher to become uncomfortable enough to drop the question or answer it. Unfortunately, that reaction deprives the learners of the opportunity to participate more actively in the learning process and makes it harder for the instructor to motivate and challenge the learners.

Answer Questions

At some point during a presentation you may want to ask the learners to take five minutes to ask you questions — and if the questions are good, say so! In fact, you may want to jot down the better questions so review them if you revise your notes for future use.

If you can't answer a question adequately, admit it. Then write down the question in your notes and promise to get an answer as soon as possible. After the session or even during a break, if possible, find the answer. Then as soon as possible after you get an answer, share it with the class: "During the last session, Jorge asked a good question, one I couldn't answer. I've now got the answer." Give the answer and then thank the learner who asked you. After all, because of that question, you now know more than before.

(This is most important. Never try to fake an answer or evade a question. It's not honest and it disrespects the learners. As a subject matter expert, you may feel at times like the learners expect you to know everything. Maybe they do, but they also know you're human.)

Just before taking a break, direct the learners to take two minutes to write out a question about the content you've presented, a question that was not asked and answered completely. Collect and review their questions before you continue the session.

Outline

In order for the learners to get the greatest benefit from a presentation, you should structure and organize it appropriately and aim it at the objectives you've set for the session and the course. It's all too easy to go off on a tangent or, especially for subject matter experts, to do a "brain dump" and overwhelm the learners with information they're not ready to process or may never use.

An outline is essential for a good presentation, for several reasons. Of course, it helps you structure and organize the material you want to present. It allows you to estimate better how much time will be needed to deliver the lecture. It allows and even encourages you to insert questions at appropriate points and to schedule breaks. It helps you keep on track and avoid the problem of fitting 10 minutes of material frantically into the final two minutes. You can use the outline to rehearse your presentation. Also, when you know you have an outline, you can feel more confident and have a better sense of how the session will flow.

Outline important parts, steps, and elements of the presentation. Include a summary of main facts, concepts, principles, and generalizations you wish to cover. Be sure to have any necessary materials and equipment ready — charts, maps, photographs, transparencies, slides, handouts, computer, and so on.

You can structure the presentation to follow this hierarchy of thinking (aka Bloom's taxonomy):

1. Knowledge (getting, storing, and recalling information)

2. Comprehension (understanding information)

3. Application (using information)

4. Analysis (examining, distinguishing the parts of a whole, understanding patterns and interrelationships)

5. Synthesis (forming relationships, generalizations, and conclusions)

6. Evaluation (comparing, judging, discriminating)

(For more, check "More about the Hierarchy of Thinking" at the end of this book.)

It is not necessary to be able to peg each question at a specific level. The value of this hierarchy is that it can guide you in shaping your questions and learning activities to the learners and the objectives you've set for them.

So, for example, you could provide facts early in the presentation and then work up through comprehension to application. Or you could begin by reviewing and checking understanding of material covered earlier in the course and progress into analysis and then synthesis.

Communicate Your Content

You may have a lot of subject matter expertise and you may structure your presentation most effectively, but if you don't deliver what you've got so that the learners can understand you and feel motivated to pay attention to you, you're not doing your job right.

Speak slowly and clearly. Aim your words at all areas of the room. Learners shouldn't have to strain to hear you.

Vary the pitch and tone of your voice. You're more interesting when you show you're interested in the material and in the learners.

Look at the learners, not at the board, walls, floor, or ceiling. You pick up many cues from their expressions. You may sense a need to explain something better or ask for questions.

Emphasize your points visually. This means, at the very least, writing the essence of most important points on the board or flip chart. When you write something, it sends the message that it's worth taking note.

Be prepared — but be alive, spontaneous. There's something positive about spontaneity that keeps learners attentive. Spontaneity is an art to develop and to balance with the science of preparation. You want to be prepared, but not so much that you squelch spontaneity.

Provide illustrations and examples from current events, from the world in which they work and live. Remember: adult learners are practical. They want learning to be relevant to their lives and their work, their needs, interests, activities, goals, and problems.

Don't just stand there. Move your body as well as your mouth. Adults question the confidence and preparation of instructors who stand with white knuckles at a podium day after day. If you don't feel relaxed and confident in front of a group, you may want to seek advice — if you're in an academic setting, from instructors in speech communication and theater arts or, if you're in a business setting, from trainers and from colleagues who give professional presentations.

Demonstration

If any of your behavioral objectives involve doing something, as opposed to recalling and using knowledge, then demonstrations may be appropriate.

If you expect the learners to learn how to use a tool, a software program, or a machine, for example, you could show them how. The following would be a natural and logical progression of instructional strategies:

- You explain.

- You answer questions and you ask questions.

- You demonstrate.

- You answer questions and you ask questions.

- Learners practice.

- You answer questions and you ask questions.

It's simple: you tell, you show, they do, with questions and answers to bridge any gaps.

Discussion

Discussions have many advantages. They usually motivate better than lectures — although a dynamic and well-orchestrated lecture will probably be more motivational than a poorly planned and disorganized discussion.

They are best suited for objectives that deal with higher cognitive processes (refer back to Bloom's taxonomy) and problem-solving activities. You should consider using the discussion approach when your objectives include having learners formulate and solve problems, providing them opportunities to draw upon their experiences.

Ask Questions

You can develop questions to generate discussion and engage learners in thinking if you use the four higher-level skills of

Bloom's taxonomy — application, analysis, synthesis, and evaluation — as a guide.

Application questions. These questions push the learner beyond than the simple recall of information. The purpose of these questions is to lead learners to apply concepts, principles, and information in different contexts. For example:

- How would the concept of product life cycle help us to market more effectively?

- Considering what we've been learning about the political structures of local government, how would you start if you wanted to get a stop sign installed on your street?

- If I gave you a comma-separated values text file of 100 records (names, addresses, and current property assessment), how would you bring that data into Excel, alphabetize the records by last name, and calculate the average property value?

Analysis questions. These questions require a deeper understanding, often involving comparing, contrasting, categorizing. For example:

- What is the central idea of Freudian psychology?

- List the four main principles of socialism.

- Compare these two computers in terms of long-term costs, ease of use, and reliability.

- What is the biggest advantage of NAFTA for the average citizen of the United States? What is the biggest disadvantage?

Synthesis questions. These questions pulling together information and going beyond — solving problems, inventing, creating, predicting, imagining. For example:

- Considering what you know about this community, where would you locate a large retail mall and why?

- How are interest rates for short-term business loans from commercial banks related to the U.S. Prime Rate?

- How could Americans be encouraged to save more money?

Questions that call for evaluation. There are generally no right or wrong answers to evaluation questions. This type of question requires using the other cognitive processes — knowledge, comprehension, application, analysis, and synthesis — and going beyond.

For example:

- Which of these three suggested solutions is best, and why?

- What would be the most effective way to solve the problem of global warming?

- Evaluate the manufacturing strategy of just-in-time in terms of the likely long-range effects on vendors.

One of the keys to engaging learners in discussions is to use probing questions, especially asking, "Why?" If you ask a question and you receive a "Yes" or "No" or a simplistic response, follow up with "Why?" This forces learners to reveal their reasons and thought processes, their knowledge and their sources of information, and to develop an ability to think at higher levels and communicate their thoughts.

Use Case Studies

Case studies are basically developed story problems. Using them can be appropriate when the session objectives include encouraging the learners to analyze, synthesize, and evaluate.

You provide the learners with a scenario, giving them enough background information so they can apply basic concepts and principles. Then you ask a series of questions.

When you use case studies, you should present the scenario and then move out of the way. Focus on encouraging the learners to take over and work with the scenario, guiding them toward more active, thoughtful involvement.

Cooperative Learning Activities

In cooperative learning, learners work on assignments as teams. The ideal is to create an atmosphere of "positive interdependence" in which the learners interact and help each other, with a sense of individual and team accountability, and develop interpersonal and teamwork skills.

Cooperative learning should respect the differences that exist among the members of any group. It encourages communication and teamwork, because it requires interaction.

How do you encourage cooperative learning? Form groups, trying to ensure a mix in each of ability levels and personalities. How many members in a group? Between three and six or seven, depending largely on the activity. Then you could try the following:

- Assign questions for the learners to work together to answer.

- Give a topic to each group and ask the members to prepare a report, which they will present in class.

- Ask the groups to each prepare five questions about the subject covered in that session, which they will ask of the members of the other groups.

Always specify the goal of the activity, set a time, and state any expectations or rules. The better the learners understand what they should be doing, the less time and energy they'll spend trying to agree on what to do. Provide assistance if needed and only as much as needed.

Experiential Activities

In experiential activities, as mentioned earlier, learners actually do something. The most common experiential activities would include simulations, hands-on learning activities, and field experiences.

Simulations

Traditional simulations are closely allied to case studies. They consist basically of enacting or staging some real-life situation or event. They are particularly useful when session or course objectives include recognizing and appreciating the values and attitudes of other groups and cultures.

To set up a simulation, obtain as much information as possible about the situation or event and the people. Set up the simulation by establishing structure and rules and by providing materials. Then cast learners to play the roles.

Be sure to explain how the activity relates to your objectives. Involve as many learners as feasible; you may want to do the same situation several times, rotating the roles among the learners. Then conduct a discussion. You should prepare in advance a list of the points that you want to discuss; if the learners do not bring up those points, you're ready to interject them.

Technology has redefined "simulation." A computer simulation creates a virtual reality. The world of simulations is vast and expanding — too vast to cover here. If you use a computer simulation, you can develop the potential for learning with discussion in advance and after the simulation. To find appropriate simulations, search the Web and ask colleagues.

Hands-on Learning Activities

These activities provide learners with opportunities to apply their knowledge in a real-world environment and practice skills in direct learning experiences. In academic settings, these are traditionally called "labs." In business settings, learning labs may have various names. (One company calls its learning lab the "marketer's sandbox.")

These learning activities are appropriate for objectives that involve research methods, application, and observation skills. They can involve conducting experiments, observing demonstrations, collecting data, designing and pursuing projects, and so on. These experiences often provide opportunities for autonomy and individual responsibility, require personal initiative, and help develop decision-making skills. Of course, as technology develops, the line between virtual experiences and real-world practice continues to blur.

You no doubt are familiar with hands-on learning activities in academic settings, as courses in many disciplines include labs and similar experiences. There are possibilities as well in business environments, for example:

- If you're training in technology with which the learners are unfamiliar, such as software or the company intranet or telephone system, they could practice working with it.

- If you're training customer service representatives in a company that sells equipment, you could send them out with the people who install the equipment so they can get direct exposure to the problems that customers experience.

- If you're training volunteers in a nonprofit organization, you could have them do an "internship" of an hour or two in each of the organization's offices or divisions.

Field Experiences

It may be relevant to your course objectives to provide the learners with a field experience, a trip outside the usual learning environment. You probably went on school field trips when you were young. They can be appropriate for learning at any age.

Here are some examples of field experiences that could be a part of business training:

In a business environment:

- If you're training new marketers and/or salespeople on the company's product line, you could take them on a tour of the factory where they are produced and/or send them to stores that sell your company's products to talk with shoppers and get their opinions about your products, the company's image, your marketing approaches, and so on.

- If you're training insurance agents, you could have each of the learners accompany an agent with a good sales records as he or she calls on potential customers.

Field experiences can involve liability issues. Check with your supervisor about any field experience you're considering and follow any policy or guidelines. Think about safety, scheduling, and transportation — and accessibility as well, if any learners have mobility limitations. Take the trip yourself in advance so you can better anticipate and prepare.

How could learners benefit the most from a field experience? Through a discussion? If so, on site or in the next session? What other activities might be appropriate?

Let's close this long section on selecting strategies as succinctly as possible: use strategies that are most effective in helping the learners achieve your course and session objectives, that respect the principles of adult learning, and that are varied to work for all learning styles — visual, auditory, and tactile/kinesthetic.

SELECT THE MATERIALS

Materials may include a schedule (agenda or syllabus), hand-outs, visuals (slides, transparencies, charts, photographs, etc.), books, *realia* (Latin for "things"), audio recordings, videos, Web site, e-mail, and so on — whatever physical or virtual means you use to help learners understand the subject matter.

Here are four basic criteria. Materials should be:

- *Effective*: Materials should help the students learn — not confuse them, not distract them.

- *Efficient*: Materials should be effective without requiring excessive time and effort of the learners. If you give them an article that contains only some passages relevant to the subject, mark those passages so they can skip the rest. If you use slide presentations, show only the slides that are relevant to the subject and most effective. (You may be familiar with "death by Power-Point" and "data dumping." A word to the wise ….)

- *Varied*: Remember that people learn in different ways. And even if all of the learners are visual, don't limit your materials to handouts or slides, for example.

- *Professional*: If you use materials with any text, make sure the grammar and punctuation are at least acceptable and the spelling is correct. If you would not submit the materials to your supervisor, don't use them in your course.

Do It Yourself

Sometimes the best materials are those that you prepare specifically for the course. If you set the objectives for the course and objectives for each session, it's logical to take responsibility for preparing the materials, too.

Here are some guidelines for whatever materials you prepare:

- Focus on your session and course objectives.

- Provide what the learners need — the practical stuff.

- Communicate clearly. Whether you're using words or graphics, think about how well they will convey to the learners what you want to convey.

- Avoid bias — gender, racial, ethnic, religious, and so on. If you're unsure about the language you're using on handouts and other materials, check with colleagues and friends.

- Balance perspectives. If there are different theories or approaches, for example, give equal and fair treatment to each of them.

Two points about handouts: purpose and timing.

If a handout accompanies a presentation, try to make it complementary rather than the same or similar. It should help learners understand the presentation, not encourage them to pay less attention to you and to not take notes.

Think about when to distribute your handout — before the presentation, during, or after? Is it likely to distract them? Will you want to be referring to it? Would it help them follow your presentation?

Borrow — with Care

You may not be totally free to prepare materials and/or you may not have the time and/or the expertise to do so. In that case, like many instructors, you may compile the most appropriate materials from various sources. If you do so, then at least adapt whatever materials are assigned, given, or borrowed.

That last word, "borrowed," brings us into a dangerous area — and adds a fifth criterion to the four listed above: materials should be legal.

If you find a particularly good article or illustration that's copyrighted, get permission to use it. If you find it in a book or a periodical, obtain permission from the author and publishing company. If you find it online, obtain permission from the author or whoever holds the copyright. This is a question of professional ethics, of course, but there are also legal risks that could prove costly.

Copyright is subject to certain limitations (Copyright Act, U.S. Code, title 17, sections 107–118). One that most people recognize is *fair use*. This doctrine may apply in teaching. There are four factors used in determining whether a particular use is fair or not. The first is whether the use is commercial or for nonprofit educational purposes; this factor may rule out fair use for training and in some situations for teaching.

You have two choices. You can read this section of the law very carefully ... and be prepared to find a good attorney, just in case — or you can get permission for anything that is copyrighted.

The page of the book or periodical that contains the copyright notice shows the copyright owner, the year of publication, and the publisher. If the copyright owner is the author or another publisher, you must request permission from that person or company. The address of the publisher is often in the book or periodical. If not, you may find it (for books) in the *American Booksellers Association's Publishers Directory* or *Books in Print* or (for periodicals) *Ulrich's International Periodicals Directory*. These references can be found in most libraries.

The American Association of Publishers recommends including the following information in your letter to request permission:

- Title, author and/or editor, and edition of the material that you want to use

- Exact material to be used — page numbers or other specifics

- How you intend to use the material

- Form of distribution (e.g., classroom, seminar, Web site, newsletter, etc.) and, if you intend to photocopy or print the material, the number of copies

- Whether or not the material is to be sold

Mail your request with a self-addressed stamped envelope to the permissions department of the publisher. (If you must have permission immediately, you can try calling or e-mailing to make contact and then faxing your request for a signature. However, it's good to have the signed document for your files.)

Be More than Just a Talking Text

If you're using a book or a handout, it's best not to just repeat the exact words of that text. An instructor should always be adding value to his or her materials. Instructors who merely read a text aloud are wasting opportunities — and indirectly encouraging learners not to read. They are undermining motivation, participation, enthusiasm — and learning.

If the text is one that the learners were expected to read, then try asking questions about it or asking them to summarize sections of it. If the text is new to them, you could suggest which points are most important or give them questions to answer while reading it.

(We offer recommendations for using materials in the section, "Use Instructional Media Effectively.")

PLAN EACH SESSION

In sketching out your schedule, you decided what areas to cover in each session in order for the learners to achieve the course objectives. Now, in planning each session, you need to decide what you mean by "cover."

Start by Setting Objectives

Ask yourself, "What do I want the learners to be able to do at the end of this session?" You should answer this question by setting objectives. Your objectives for each session should be aligned with your objectives for the course.

Session objectives, like course objectives, should be expressed in terms of what learners will be expected to do. However, unlike course objectives, which may specify conditions and performance standards, it's not necessary for session objectives to be that specific, unless you intend to use them for a test at the end of the session. It's generally sufficient for session objectives to state in general terms what the learners will be able to do at the end of the session.

- You will be able to create and save a spreadsheet.

- You will be familiar with the five phases of Six Sigma (DMAIC) and what happens during each phase.

- You will know how to read a profit and loss statement.

- You will understand the purpose of the Pareto diagram and how to use one.

It's best if you write no more than a half-dozen objectives for a one–hour session. You can overwhelm the learners if you give them a lot of objectives.

Then, once you've identified the objectives for that session, ask yourself, "Which strategies would probably be most effective in terms of those objectives?"

One way to develop activities is by thinking in terms of Bloom's taxonomy. For each behavioral objective:

- Decide what level of cognitive skill is involved to achieve that objective.

- Determine the current level of the learners with respect to that specific area of information targeted by that objective.

- Determine the steps that you must take so the learners can move from their current level to the level of the objective.

Here's an example.

You're teaching Intro to Bookkeeping. One of your objectives for the session is "You will know how to journalize entries." (In behavioral terms, this might be "Given a list of 20 business transactions and a chart of accounts, learners will journalize the transactions." If you wanted to use this objective to evaluate the learners, you would set conditions and performance levels.)

To achieve this objective, students must understand the principles of double-entry bookkeeping, the structure of a chart of accounts, the structure of a general ledger, and the meaning of "debit" and "credit."

- What level of cognitive skill is involved? They must know, they must understand, and they must apply the principles. The highest level, then, is application.

- At what level are the learners currently? You've pre-sented the basics, but they have not yet shown they understand and can apply them.

- What steps must you take? You need to ensure that they understand those basics and you need to allow them to practice using them.

Decide on Activities

Now you decide on the activities to take the learners through those steps so they can achieve the objective. It may take a progres-sion of several activities for each step, especially to ensure variety. You should generally review material before you work with it at a higher cognitive level.

In this example, your first activity might be asking the learn-ers to define and/or explain the concepts and terms. This activity would ensure that they understand the basics. You might allot five minutes for this activity. The next activity might be to involve the learners in "dissecting" transactions and explaining why account X is debited and account Y is credited. You might do a half-dozen transactions at the board or on a flip chart until you feel they're be-coming comfortable with journalizing. You might allot eight min-utes for this. The third activity might be the same, but you would make it cooperative by dividing the learners into groups of three and putting up a transparency or a chart describing a half-dozen transactions. You might allow the groups eight minutes. You would follow up by taking the transactions one by one and asking the groups how they journalized each of them and why. You might allot five minutes for this follow-up. Your next step might be to give a quiz based on your objective: you could hand out three sheets to each participant: one describing 20 business transac-tions, one showing a simple chart of accounts, and one showing a page from a general journal. You might allow them 10 minutes to journalize the transactions. You could collect the quizzes, run through the transactions at the board or on the flip chart, or both. That could take five minutes, more if they have questions. In that case, turn each question around to the group; answer it only if no learner can do so.

So, you've outlined six activities, for a total of 41 minutes. List them in order, indicate the time for each (and maybe the start and end times), and note any materials you'll need. Here's an example:

questions: define/explain list of terms	5	10:00-10:05
transactions (whole class) half-dozen transactions	8	10:05-10:13
transactions (groups of 3) half-dozen transactions (chart)	8	10:13-10:21
follow-up (whole class)	5	10:21-10:26
quiz handout: 20 transactions, chart of accounts, general journal page	10	10:26-10:36
follow-up (whole class)	5	10:36-10:41

Your session plan should be in whatever format works for you. The important thing is to plan the distribution of time and the variety of activities and methods.

If the course will take more than 50 minutes or an hour, consider scheduling a break so the learners and can use the rest rooms, get some water or refreshments, smoke (wherever it's permitted), check phone messages, make phone calls, and so on. It may reassure them and reduce distractions if you tell them at the beginning of the session when you've scheduled a break.

First Session

What should you plan and prepare for the first session? In addition to learning activities and any materials, of course, here are some other possibilities:

- your introduction (notes or practice)
- the course objectives (notes or handout)
- any course rules/expectations (notes or handout)
- the course schedule (handout)

Timing may be more difficult for the first session, so make your plans flexible enough to allow for a lot of questions … or no questions, for passive learners … or talkative learners, and so on. Plan more activities than you expect to need: extra questions, extra examples — things that you can drop if time runs short.

Here's an activity that can provide a great start for the course and help establish a good relationship with the learners. Ask the learners to identify the things they expect to learn from the course. List their expectations on a flip chart. At the end of the first session, save those sheets. Then, as you plan each session, review the listed expectations. How many are you addressing? Are there others that you should or could address?

Know What to Put In and What to Leave Out

We all love our subject matter areas. But that can be a problem if we assume that the learners in our courses feel the same way — or we don't even think about how they feel or what they need.

Subject matter experts in the roles of trainers and teachers may tend to make these mistakes:

- They neglect to explain or maybe even to mention basic information or basic instructions.

- They include every detail and naturally overwhelm or confuse the learners.

- They discuss the situations and problems they find most interesting, generally the least common, instead of situations and problems that learners are most likely to encounter.

Again, focus on the behavioral objectives you've set, for the course and for each session. What do the learners need in order to achieve those objectives?

Again, allow time for questions — both to answer and to ask.

Plan Transitions

Finally, you may want to plan how you'll transition from one activity into the next. It might be with just a simple sentence, e.g., "OK, now we'll do this same exercise, but in groups." It might be a little more involved, e.g., "We've talked about X, we've discussed Y, and we've discussed Z. Now we're going to get into how the three are interrelated."

Transitions are good in that they help the learners follow what's happening. They're also good when you're planning, because thinking about transitions can help you realize when you're moving from one activity into another that's much more difficult and you should plan an intermediate activity to help the learners bridge the gap.

Plan an Introduction

After you've planned the activities for a session, you should think about how you'll start the session. That can be important, because the right beginning can guide and motivate the learners and show that you're organized.

You can share the objectives you've set for the session or simply give a general idea of what the session will cover. You can make connections between what was covered in previous sessions and what will be covered in the session you're beginning. You can finish things left unfinished, answer questions that have arisen since the previous session, and review and reinforce things that are important and/or relevant to the session you're beginning (as in the example given above).

You may want to prepare an advance organizer. This is a cognitive instructional strategy used to help learners learn and retain new information by providing a bridge to connect known information with new information. Advance organizers are broad, goal-oriented statements or assignments that help learners prepare mentally for a session. You might make a simple statement before a presentation, e.g., "Today, we will discuss exponential functions." You might give a short reading assignment about the topic, but lacking specifics.

First Session

The first session of the course is the most important. As the saying goes, "You never get a second chance to make a first impression."

You should prepare to begin the first session this way:

- *How will you introduce yourself?* Decide what you'll tell the learners about yourself: your name, of course, and some background — professional and, if you choose, personal.

- *How will you have the learners introduce themselves?* Decide what you what you want them to include:

e.g., their names, current work activities, reasons for taking the course, etc.

- *How will you describe the course in general terms?* Decide what you're going to say. Prepare notes so you can do it succinctly and not forget anything.

- *What are the course objectives?* Prepare notes and maybe a display, such as slides, transparencies, or flip chart pages. You could also include these on the course schedule.

- *What rules or expectations should you set?* These might include behavior in class, use of outside materials, and so on. You should probably also state these on the course schedule.

- *Does the course schedule provide all necessary information so that the learners can understand?* Review it from their perspective.

Attend to the Details

Finally, pack up all of your materials — notes, handouts, computer, slides, transparencies, charts, maps, photographs, etc. Make sure that all is ready to grab and go. Running around at the last moment, arriving late, forgetting things — that makes it tougher to do a good job and enjoy what you're doing.

Also, make sure you'll have whatever equipment you'll need — e.g., overhead projector, microphone, laptop computer, slide projector, film projector.

First Session

Check out the facilities. How is the size of the room? How are the acoustics from various locations? How well will the learners be able to see anything you display — boards, flip chart, or whatever? You could ask another person to sit in various seats to give you perspectives.

Make sure your equipment is ready for you — and you're ready for your equipment:

- Check that you'll have whatever equipment you'll need — e.g., overhead projector, microphone, laptop computer, slide projector, film projector.

- Know how to use the equipment. Practice with it, if possible.

Know whom to contact for immediate assistance in case of equipment problems.

Attending to such details will take some extra time, but the results will justify your investment. You'll be better prepared — and more confident.

START INSTRUCTING!

Arrive prepared and early — at least five minutes, 10 if possible. Be approachable from the start: as the learners arrive, make eye contact, smile, and welcome them. Be human. Some instructors play music while the learners are entering the classroom. When the music stops, it cues the adults that the session is about to begin. Others project a cartoon onto the screen and then, when they start the session, relate the cartoon to what they are planning to cover in the session.

Start on time. Show that you respect their time. If you start on time, they will know that you mean business and they will try harder to get there on time for future sessions.

First Session

Introduce yourself. Give your name and a little background: experience in the subject matter area, experience teaching or training. Show that you're enthusiastic not only about the subject but about the opportunity to help them learn about it. You may also choose to provide some personal background — but keep it brief.

Have the learners introduce themselves. They can give their names, tell what they do "in the outside world," and maybe tell why they're taking the course.

It's important to call on learners by their names, if possible. You could take notes as each introduces himself or herself, jotting a description. You could also hand out cards folded in half and ask them to write out their names and set the cards in front of them.

After the learners have all introduced themselves, introduce them to the course. Describe it in general terms. State the course objectives, displaying them if you've prepared to do so. (Studies have revealed significant increases in learning when people hear or receive in writing a set of objectives in behavioral terms prior to instruction.)

As mentioned earlier, adult learners are goal-oriented and they need to be autonomous. Even if it's impossible to allow them autonomy, you should involve them actively in the course objectives. They may offer suggestions for shaping more appropriately the objectives you've set and they may suggest other objectives. The way you work with the people in your course from the start in determining how the course will work sends a strong message. We're not advising you to scrap your objectives, but only to involve the learners in finalizing the objectives according to their perceived needs.

Hand out the course schedule and review it briefly. Explain any rules, expectations, and policies.

Next, you might want to get a better sense of who the learners are. Ask them to each write on a sheet of paper their name and their goals for the course — what they expect to get out of it in terms of their current needs. Collect the sheets and review them later; they may guide you in planning the sessions, particularly in choosing activities, materials, and examples.

You may also want to find out what they know. A simple way is by asking questions. It's important to get correct answers, of course — but even more important to watch how the learners react when one of them gives a correct answer. Observe their expressions. Do they seem surprised or confused by the answer? Or do they seem reassured and confident? Do any of them take notes, as if what you expect them to know is new or at least not very familiar?

Ease into the Work

Transition into learning activities smoothly. It's great to be enthusiastic about what you're doing, but too much too early can overwhelm and even put off learners. People usually learn better when they feel more comfortable and they generally feel less comfortable if you jump into an activity abruptly. This is especially true early on, before they know you at all.

You could tell a story about yourself, one that shows your human side — e.g., a goof that you made, something you forgot to do, a special event like a wedding anniversary. Share something from *The Wall Street Journal*, *The New York Times*, or a local newspaper. Tell them an anecdote. Just take the first few minutes to ease the learners into the work.

As suggested earlier, you may want to use an advance organizer.

It can also help if you tell the learners your objectives for the session and perhaps display them on a board, a flip chart, a transparency, or a slide. As mentioned earlier, adult learners are goal-oriented. Just put it simply, e.g., "By the end of this session you will be able to …." As mentioned earlier, it's best to have at most a half-dozen objectives, so you don't overwhelm the learners or spend a lot of time sharing the objectives. If you put the objectives on display, during the session you can point to an objective from time to time to emphasize the connection between content and objectives.

First Session

You may want to start the first session by finding out what the learners know and can do. This establishes interactivity from the start and it helps you know where and how to start presenting material. Begin by asking them questions about facts, terms, and concepts. Then you may want to present some simple application problems.

Show a Sense of Humor ...
or at Least a Human Side

Books on teaching or training usually advise showing a sense of humor. This does not mean that you should tell jokes. It just means that you can be serious about the subject matter and teaching or training without being a zombie or a robot.

If you decide to tell jokes or just joke around, don't try for humor at the expense of anyone but yourself. It's no laughing matter if your humor is offensive.

First Session

Go easy on the humor until you get to know the learners: don't give the impression you're more interested in entertaining them than helping them learn. Learners may be nervous and tentative, so be sensitive and read their faces.

You may be feeling anxious and/or feeling anxiety among the learners. You may feel like joking to reduce the anxiety and they may laugh because of the anxiety. This is OK and natural, but avoid doing too much of it.

Act, React, Interact

What you do next is follow the plan you've developed for the lesson. But it's advisable to try to balance the P's:

- Plan: This is your map for getting from point A to point B.

- People: These learners are your reason for doing what you're doing.

- Personality: The particular atmosphere of the learning environment should make the learners feel comfortable, confident, and challenged.

All three are important and you should be sensitive to developing a feel for the proper balance. And, as we advised earlier, be prepared — but be open to being spontaneous.

If you're doing a presentation, move around the room — without becoming a distraction. This gets you out and among the learners. If they don't feel distant from you, it should be easier for them to ask and answer questions. It also helps you hold their attention better.

Encourage the learners to interact with you. Ask a question and then pause — perhaps as long as five to 10 seconds — before calling on someone to answer. As we emphasized earlier, be patient: allow enough time to think about the question and formulate an answer.

Praise learners when they give appropriate answers: "That's a great response" or "That answer is particularly important because ...." Be specific: specify why the answer is good. Avoid praising every answer, especially generally; if you get into the habit of saying "Good answer" or "Good idea" to every response or comment, the learners will quickly realize your praise is empty.

If someone gives an incorrect response, there are several ways you could react.

- Turn to another person and ask if he or she agrees with that response and then follow up with "Why?" or "Why not?" The person giving the incorrect response is less likely to feel embarrassed as you use the answer to generate a short discussion.

- If it's possible that the learner misunderstood your question, say something like "I may have phrased the question poorly" or "Let me word the question a little differently." Do so and then choose another learner to answer.

- If the answer is not incorrect, but just not the best answer or not the answer you wanted, say something like "That's correct, although there are other possibilities" or "I didn't expect that answer, but it's correct." Then ask the class, "What other possible ways could we answer that question?" You might want to write the answers on the board or flip chart.

- If the answer is partly correct or at least uses some appropriate words, say something like "OK, now we have part of the answer" or "Now we're getting close to the answer." Write those words on the board or flip chart. Then ask the class, "Who can help us get a little closer?"

It's generally not good to simply reject an answer — "No." It's also not good to say, "That's not what I had in mind" or "That's not what I wanted," since it implies that learners should guess at what you want, like it's a game.

Encourage the learners to ask questions. Start doing this in the first session. Check their understanding. Don't ask questions such as "Do you understand?" or "OK?" The tendency is then to simply nod. Ask the learners for specifics, e.g., "What does Y mean?" or "How could we use A?" and "Why would B be important?"

When someone asks a question, acknowledge it immediately. Repeat it if you're not sure the others have heard it. Depending on the question, answer it yourself or invite the others to answer it. It may be appropriate to do both; for example, if the question is "How do we froozle the widget?" and you explain that there are two ways, you might ask the others to identify situations in which the first way would be best and situations in which the second would be preferred.

Close the Session

It is important to end the session by summarizing and emphasizing the key points. The final moments are best used to consolidate what was covered in the session and prepare the learners for the next session. If you try to squeeze in additional information, it does not benefit the learners as much as if you reiterate the most important material.

Another way to close the session is with a quick evaluation. Ask the learners to rate the session in terms of the session objectives you put on display at the start of the session (and which must still be on display and numbered for this evaluation):

For each of the listed objectives for this session, write the number of the objective and then how you would rate the session:

- A — This session enabled us to achieve this objective.

- B — This session helped us get closer to achieving this objective.

- C — This session helped us a little toward this objective.

- D — This session did not do much to help us achieve this objective.

- F — This session made it more difficult for us to achieve this objective.

For any objective for which you give this session a B or lower, please write down any problems and offer any suggestions.

You can also close the session is with a *minute paper*. Give the learners 60 seconds to answer anonymously one or more questions like the following:

- What was the main point of this session?

- What was the most important thing you learned during this session?

- What question do you wish the instructor had answered or in what area do you think the instructor should have spent more time?

Collect the papers. The answers should give you a good sense for how well you covered the material and what points you should review and/or emphasize at the start of the next session.

You could also give the learners a little more time and ask them to name the thing that you did that worked best for them and the thing that they thought was least effective.

End on time. This is important because some of the learners will have other commitments. As they leave, thank those who contributed the most to the class. Be brief and, as always, be specific: e.g., "Tami, great question!" or "Aaron, I was impressed with your contributions today!" Try to pick the three or four learners who most helped the session work.

FOLLOW UP ON EACH SESSION

Elicit Reactions from Learners

In addition to or instead of eliciting comments toward the end of the session, you could ask for feedback after the session. Select three learners to meet with you briefly at the close of the session. Ask them questions such as these:

- How are the other learners progressing?

- Are there any problems so far?

- What do you think worked best in this session?

- What to you think worked least well?

- Did the material covered seem relevant and practical?

Take notes. Even if you're sure you'll remember all their comments, take notes. It sends the message that you're taking their input seriously. Then use their reactions to improve what you're doing.

Evaluate Yourself

You should follow up each session by evaluating yourself. A quick and simple way is by answering the following questions:

- What did I do well in this session?

- What could I have done better?

- What could I have done to be more effective?

- How well did I engage the learners?

- Which activities seemed to work best?

- Which activities were least effective?

- What things should I do differently the next time?

Take notes on how you answer those questions. Mark on your session schedule and in any presentation notes. You want to improve your methods for the remaining sessions in the course and for instructing that course or others in the future. Record your feelings and concerns and ideas while they're fresh.

MOTIVATE

Don't expect all adult learners to be motivated by the same factors and to the same extent. As we mentioned earlier, one of the key characteristics of adult learners is that they differ widely by their knowledge and their life and work experience as well as by the factors listed by Stephen Brookfield: "differences of class, culture, ethnicity, personality, cognitive style, learning patterns, life experiences, and gender."

However, generally the characteristics of adult learners presented earlier can help you train or teach in ways that will motivate the learners in your course.

Keep in Mind the Characteristics of Adult Learners

Adult learners are practical.

- Always present the big picture before getting into details. Then conclude by returning to the big picture.

- Relate theories and concepts to the learners' experiences and work situations.

- Emphasize ways in which they can apply what they're learning.

- Make sure they understand why they're doing the activities you plan.

- Validate and use their work experience.

- Tell them, "Your experiences are valuable. Share them with your colleagues." Remind them of this especially before cooperative learning activities or discussions.

Some learners may not feel motivated to participate in these activities because they think they can't learn much from each other or at least not as efficiently as with you, the subject matter expert.

Adult learners are goal-oriented.

- Find out their reasons for taking the course.

- Give them the course objectives at the start of the course.

- Make sure that each session and all your activities are aimed at the course objectives.

- Provide information according to the course objectives. If information doesn't help them achieve those objectives, is it relevant? Facts that you consider important might seem like trivia to learners who don't perceive any need for those facts.

- Present material that's relevant to their situations, as close to work requirements as possible.

- Explain the reasons for any assignments in terms of the course objectives.

Adult learners differ widely by their knowledge and their life and work experience.

- Use various approaches and strategies.

- Provide examples that connect with their experiences and areas of knowledge.

- Be appreciative when you learn something from them. That's the right attitude in a learning environment — and it can be a great motivator.

- Maintain an appropriate balance between variety and routine. Don't bore them — but also don't confuse them or distract their attention and energy from pursuing the objectives.

Adult learners need to be autonomous, free to direct themselves.

- Involve them actively in shaping the course objectives to better fit their needs.

- Give them opportunities to work in groups and to assume responsibility for presentations.

- Allow them freedom in assignments, in whatever ways possible.

Adult learners demand respect.

- Acknowledge the value of their experience and knowledge.

- Connect what they're learning to what they know already.

- Ask for examples and applications from their work experience.

- Treat them as your peers. Never act in any way that could be considered condescending. Also, don't deliberately use vocabulary that they might not understand — don't show off.

- Allow them to express their opinions freely.

- Use their time effectively and efficiently. Start and end on time.

- Allow breaks so they can use the rest rooms, walk around, drink something, eat something, make phone calls, and check for messages.

- Avoid using jargon or other words you're not sure they'll all understand.

- Ask them to let you know how you're doing. That attitude shows that you care and respect their opinions.

Consider Other General Factors

There are other factors that affect the motivation of the learners in your course.

1. They have other responsibilities, both work and personal. Any assignments you give them to do outside of class must compete with those responsibilities for their time and energy.

   - Minimize the time they must spend on assignments outside of class.

   - Make any assignments as relevant as possible to their work responsibilities.

   - Specify how long you expect an assignment will take. For example, "Write the answers to the questions on the handout. Be complete — maybe 50-75 words for each answer. It should take you probably between 20 and 40 minutes."

   - Let them know how well to prepare for a session. For example, don't tell them only, "Read pages 27-43." Tell them why: "You should understand the points presented on pp. 32-35 well enough to discuss them. I'll be going over the material on pp. 39-43 in class.

It's a little tough, so don't worry if you don't understand it. Write down any questions that come to mind."

2. They're accustomed to doing, to being active, not passive.

- Take breaks more frequently, at least two minutes to stand up and stretch. How often? Judge from their expressions, body language, and energy levels.

- Emphasize interactive learning methods.

- Don't expect them to just "take dictation" as you lecture. Expect them to think. Use activities that involve their heads, not just their hands.

3. They're accustomed to working under a boss, not with an instructor, among co-workers, not classmates.

- Be sensitive to their sense of self-esteem.

- Plan for encouraging and supporting success by working from what they know into what they do not know.

- Help them use what they're learning and develop their skills by taking them step by step up the hierarchy of thinking (Bloom's taxonomy). (For more, check "More about the Hierarchy of Thinking" at the end of this book.)

4. They probably have practical reasons for taking the course.

- *It may be required.* With those learners, don't be surprised to encounter resentment, resistance, insecurity, and apathy. Show them that you are not the "enemy," that you will help them get the most out of an experience they cannot avoid.

- *It may be a key to opportunities, greater responsibilities, promotion.* Expect those learners to work hard and be very focused on their goals. Make sure they understand the relevance of all you do in terms of those goals.

- *It may be for personal growth and/or enjoyment.* If so, great! But unless all of the learners are in the course for this reason, don't take it into consideration when planning or instructing. Don't expect an interest in learning; expect a focus on increasing knowledge and developing skills for work.

5. They don't like to memorize.

- Reduce anxiety by providing information on handouts. This also reduces the energy required to take notes. It may make more sense to them if you provide the information in a printed form and they can then add marginal notes.

- Tell them when they do not need to memorize information — and tell them when it's necessary to memorize. Don't expect them to guess.

Find Out about the Learners as Individuals

You can go beyond generalities and motivate the learners in your course in terms of what you know about them as individuals.

Earlier we suggested several ways to find out about the people in your course. What you learn you can use to motivate them.

Have them introduce themselves — and take notes as they do. Just by asking them to introduce themselves and share their reasons for taking the course, you're motivating them by showing that you care about them as individuals and what they want and need.

Also, what they share about their situations, both work and personal, will reveal factors that motivate them and factors that might make it difficult for them to learn. And, of course, you can call on individuals by name whenever possible.

Ask them to each give you a sheet of paper with his or her goals for the course in terms of his or her specific situation. You can do more specifically what we advised doing generally: provide examples that connect with their experiences and areas of knowledge, validate and use their work experience, and ask for examples and applications from their work experience.

Ask questions to find out what they know about the subject matter. You learn what they know, of course — and how they feel about it: confident, anxious, enthusiastic, unsure, afraid ....

Motivate from the Start

Don't think of motivation as a remedy, something you do when you suspect problems. It's a preventive: it's important from the start of the course, from the moment you begin greeting the learners as they arrive.

Keep it real. The less the learning environment differs from their real world, the better. The more human *you* can be, the better. The more human you allow the *learners* to be, the better.

Establish rapport with the learners. They're with you because you know a lot and they need to learn. So, there's a sense of disparity. It helps reduce the difference if they know about you as a person.

Show that you're flexible, curious, and imaginative. These traits may motivate learners to take a greater interest in the subject matter.

Ease into the session naturally. We've suggested several ways to do this. Make them comfortable while getting their attention and arousing their interest.

Show that you've planned and organized and prepared for each session, as we advised earlier. That should make learners more confident that the course will not be wasting their time.

Motivate through maintaining a balance of comfort and challenge. Help the learners feel confident, but keep them from becoming complacent. Aim for an appropriate level of difficulty — high enough to challenge but not so high as to frustrate. Don't bore them and don't scare them. People generally learn best under low to moderate stress. If the material is very important, it may be appropriate to raise the level of stress, perhaps by asking more difficult questions. However, if it's too high, stress becomes a barrier and undermines motivation.

Encourage participation; try not to force it. We all react to situations in our own ways. Some people are naturally quiet. Some people lack confidence. Some people are enthusiastic even if they're often wrong. Some people know things but hesitate to show it. You're responsible for helping each learner achieve the course objectives. That does not mean treating them all the same and expecting them to all be the same in their learning behavior.

Don't push. If a learner cannot answer a question or do an activity, pushing undermines motivation. It will not help; it can only hurt. Whatever the reasons for not being able, making the learner feel bad cannot be good.

Maintain a learning environment that feels safe and supportive. Learners should feel free to ask questions, to admit to not knowing something, to tell you they're confused, and to let you know if the course is not meeting their expectations.

Show appreciation for good questions and good answers. Treat all questions, answers, and comments with respect. Never react to a question with comments such as "I've just explained that" or "You should know the answer to that" or with facial expressions that show frustration or ridicule or other negative emotions.

Motivate through success. Try to ensure that the learners have sufficient knowledge and skill to do cooperative learning activities and individual assignments. Don't set them up for failure.

Give the learners opportunities to show what they know. You can do this through follow-up questions. Don't probe only to find out what they *don't know*. Use questions to also allow them to show what they *know*. That reassures them, which increases motivation.

The more the learners can apply in class and on the job what they're learning, the more they're likely to feel motivated to learn. You might want to offer suggestions at the end of a session, such as "Try this at work" or "Look for examples of this at work."

Motivate by ensuring that the learners know how they're doing in relation to the course objectives and their goals. Let them know in specific terms, not general. ("Good!" is like a pat on the head. It's nice for dogs, but it generally doesn't mean much more to adult learners than "smiley face" stickers.)

You don't always have to tell them how they're doing. When you ask questions of the group, each of the learners knows how well he or she would answer those questions. You can make this activity more effective and efficient if you ask questions that require only a show of hands. Make a statement and then ask, "True or false?" Have those who believe the statement is true raise their hands. Then have those who believe the statement is false raise their hands. You can do the same with multiple-choice questions. It takes only a minute or two to ask a half-dozen questions and enable each of the learners to get a sense of how he or she is doing.

Encourage them to think, not just memorize information. That motivates them by allowing them chances to get more fully involved in the learning process. Ask questions that stretch their mental abilities. Put them into work situations with "What if ....?" questions. Be sure, however, to keep the situations grounded in their reality. Focus on preparing them for situations that are probable or at least very possible in their worlds.

Sometimes learners feel motivated just by being in a group or by working together in cooperative activities. That's not a good reason by itself for using cooperative learning — but it's a good bonus benefit. Just make sure that the cooperative groups don't engage in too much socializing or that lack of focus on learning may reduce the motivation of other learners.

Show you care about the subject matter and the learners. If you don't show you care about the *subject*, they're likely to feel less motivated to learn. If you don't show you care about *them*, they'll certainly feel less like motivated to participate in the learning process.

Be enthusiastic — but not to an extreme: Subject matter experts may find it difficult to accept that what matters so much to them may matter much less or even not at all to the learners — and that they should focus on what matters to the learners.

Learn from the Questions They Ask

Pay attention to the questions the learners ask, the questions that interest them the most. Then you can prepare for sessions more appropriately as you learn more about how they're motivated.

If they ask how the material they're learning relates to what they know already, make connections — and ask them what connections they perceive. Draw upon their knowledge and experience: it's not just a smart way to teach more effectively, but it also motivates them.

If they ask how some new information can be used, offer examples of applications. Better yet, ask them to come up with examples. Give them chances to draw on their experiences and to show how well they can think.

If they ask you to explain terms you're using, you may want to keep that in mind when you plan the sessions. Anticipate what terms might be new or unclear to them and explain those terms as you use them — and maybe not use new terms that are not essential to the material. Subject matter experts often tend to be sticklers on correct terminology, sometimes when it would be OK to use more familiar terms.

If they ask a lot of questions, consider ways to reduce questions by changing how you teach or train. Learners may feel less motivated if they must ask a lot of questions and believe that it's because of the instructor.

If they ask questions tentatively, do more to encourage questions, to answer better (maybe more specifically, maybe with fewer words, maybe in a different tone), and to thank learners who ask questions. If they feel like you welcome their questions and treat their questions as positive contributions, they should feel less reluctant to ask.

Learn from the Answers They Give

Pay attention to the answers you get from the learners. They can reveal things about the people who give them.

This may be especially true of answers that are incorrect.

If you follow up on an incorrect answer by asking, for example, "Why does that answer seem correct to you?" you can learn about a learner's perspectives and experiences. What you learn should help you present material more appropriately.

When you follow up on incorrect answers in an attempt to discover better why learners are giving them, you show that you care about what the learners know and how they think. That certainly can motivate them.

Finally, who knows? Maybe you can learn from their explanations — and maybe an answer that you thought was incorrect might actually be correct in certain situations.

> Motivation is an important factor that subject matter experts may tend to neglect. They're usually very interested in their subject area, even passionate, so they may naturally assume that the learners in their courses share that interest. Don't make this assumption.

CONSIDER USING THE SYSTEMATIC INSTRUCTION MODEL

Several decades ago, after I (Glenn Ross Johnson) did a thorough review of the literature about advance organizers, behavioral objectives, cues, positive reinforcement, and corrective feedback, I began to explore with a model for systematic teaching.

I shared the model with many colleagues. I encouraged instructors to conduct research studies in the use of the model. My colleagues and I published articles on the use of the model.

The model consists of the following steps.

Provide an *advance organizer*. Begin the session with some way of introducing the topic of the session, but without specifics. The advance organizer might consist of a short article from a newspaper or magazine on the topic of the session, but not dealing with the specifics that you will be presenting. The advance organizer might consist of a few words, such as "We have been reading articles about _____; today I want to expand on that topic." Advance organizers help the learners get ready mentally for the session.

Provide *behavioral objectives*. Present — in writing or verbally — the behavioral objectives for the lesson, so the learners know specifically what you expect of them and can learn more effectively. This also helps you teach more effectively, because it requires you to organize and plan better.

Engage the learners in the *interaction cycle*. The interaction cycle has four steps:

1. You provide directions and give cues. For example, "Be sure to record the following in your notes, because you will need to reference them after this seminar is over

and you have returned to your real world of work." In this way you highlight the importance of what you're about to present.

2. You present information, concepts, and/or generalizations for about five to 10 minutes. Limit the time you talk, so you don't exceed their attention spans without a change of pace.

3. You interject questions about the content you've just presented. This triggers "active interaction."

4. You either provide positive reinforcement ("That's a great response to my question!") or indirectly correct ("Do the others of you agree with that response?" followed up by "Why not?" or possibly "Why?).

The interaction cycle is repeated throughout the session: cue, present, ask questions about the material presented, and provide positive reinforcement or corrective feedback.

You may want to try this Systematic Instruction Model for one of your presentations to see if the learners seem to learn better and if you like using the model.

USE INSTRUCTIONAL MEDIA EFFECTIVELY

Instructional media is a big area, encompassing chalkboards and whiteboards, handouts, charts, slides, overhead transparencies, objects, video (tapes, films, DVDs), computer simulations, and on and on.

It's easy for many instructors to go crazy over instructional media — and easy for some to avoid using any. In using media, just as in selecting strategies, your choices should be guided by three considerations:

- Helping the learners achieve your course and session objectives

- Respecting the principles of adult learning

- Working for all learning styles — visual, auditory, and tactile/kinesthetic

Your choices may also be limited by the following constraints:

- resources — availability, facilities, costs, time

- personal preferences and abilities

More important than your choice of media is the way in which you use them. Here are some basic recommendations and warnings about using the basic types of instructional media more effectively.

Audio (Including Oral Presentations)

✓ Make sure that all learners can hear the material. If any cannot, suggest that they move closer to the source, if possible.

✓ Make sure the volume is at a comfortable level for all learners. That means that you should not turn the volume up for some learners if it makes others uncomfortable.

✓ Provide visual support. If you give a lecture, write the essential words on a board or flip chart. If you play an audio recording or a video with an audio track, provide a written text that includes at least the most important words.

Board or Flip Chart

✓ Face the learners when you are using the board or flip chart, even while you're writing on it. If you can't stand to the side and write, alternate writing and speaking. Avoid talking to your written words.

✓ Write in large letters, clearly and legibly, so that all can read it. If your writing is terrible, print.

✓ Write out your words; don't use short cuts to save time, unless all the learners are familiar with the shortened forms. When learners review their notes later, they should be able to understand all the words.

✓ Allow the learners enough time to take notes and to think about what you've written. If you're using a board and you need more space to continue, ask if everybody is ready for you to erase the oldest or least important of the material on the board. If you're using a flip chart, tear off the sheet on which you've written and tape it to the wall.

✓ If you intend to present material, plan ahead. What will you put where? How? Consider ways to help the learners understand your structure better: for example, you could put headings and subheads, use chalk or markers of different colors, highlight or connect with arrows, and/or write in different styles (e.g., all capitals and underlining). Make it easier for the learners to understand their notes later.

✓ If you plan how you'll display information, follow your plan. If you decide to write something you hadn't planned, try to put it away from the planned material. You're using the board as a dynamic tool, adding and changing and erasing, but the learners can't do the same with their notes.

✓ Remember that learners are generally taking notes on 8 ½ x 11" sheets of paper, while you're using a board of quite different dimensions. Don't make it difficult for them to take notes they'll understand when they refer to them later.

If you're using a board:

• Avoid competing with the past. Sometimes what you put on the board may distract learners from what you're saying five minutes later. Erase when moving on from a topic — after making sure the learners have all finished taking notes on what you've written.

If you're using a whiteboard:

• Bring your own markers — more than you think you'll need.

- Use different colors for emphasis.

- If you're using a flip chart:

- Make sure it has enough blank pages for your session.

- Prepare in advance any pages that might be difficult to do in class or take too much time.

- Bring tape so you can display pages on the wall.

Transparencies

✓ Many of the recommendations that apply to using boards or flip charts also apply to using transparencies.

✓ Keep the room light enough so learners can see the notes they're writing and you can see the expressions on their faces.

✓ Keep visuals simple and make sure they can be understood by learners farthest from the screen. Use words only as necessary to support the visuals.

✓ Use words and phrases rather than sentences and paragraphs. Your transparencies should contain only the essential points; they should not be scripts for your presentation.

✓ Use color effectively. Don't overdo it.

✓ Don't fill transparencies with information. It may be best to use one transparency for each major point. For complicated material, use a series of simple transparencies.

✓ Consider using a mask so you can disclose any transparency progressively, point by point, to better hold attention. Place a sheet of thick paper or cardboard under the transparency, to cover words or graphics you want to hide from view yet allow yourself to see what's next on your transparency.

✓ Structure the words on your transparencies with headings and subheads. Use capital letters (judiciously), underlining, and different colors.

✓ Don't use a lot of transparencies. The appropriate number depends on the material to be covered, of course, and the content of the transparencies — i.e., visuals or text. (You're using too many — or at least using them too quickly — when you're leaving learners behind, frantically trying to take notes.)

✓ Move away from the projector when you do not need to point at something on a transparency. Be the instructor, not an assistant to the machine.

Slides

✓ Many of the recommendations that apply to using boards, flip charts, and transparencies also apply to using slides. However, since computer programs make it so easy to use all the colors of the rainbow and myriad fonts of all sizes and graphics and cartoon characters and so on, you should be all the more careful when creating slides.

✓ Bear in mind that "less is more." Computer programs such as PowerPoint have made it easy to use slides — and too easy to abuse them.

✓ Don't push the slides. One rule of thumb is to spend an average of two or three minutes per slide.

✓ Use slides as a guide to your presentation — and not as a script.

✓ Generate discussion around the slides. Don't let the slides take control of the class. The learners should be using their brains as well as their note-taking hands.

Videos

✓ View every film in advance. Take notes. Decide where to pause and where to fast-forward, if it's possible to do so, or to stop. Show only what's relevant to your objectives.

✓ Create an introduction, to prepare the learners and alert them to any particular important points. Also, explain how the video is relevant to the subject matter.

✓ Review any material that will be particularly important in viewing the video. Add any information or vocabulary that will be required to understand the video.

✓ Consider preparing a handout with questions to help focus the learners on the essential points.

✓ Develop discussion questions to ask when you pause the video and to follow up.

✓ Make sure that your use of the video focuses on your objectives for the session and the course.

When using any electronic media:

• Do not expect the tools to do the training or teaching for you. Always be in control of the learning environment and always keep it focused on your objectives.

- Be prepared with a backup plan, in case there's a problem. Be ready to continue without the media.

Our intent in this book is to cover the basics, so we're not getting into the technologies of teaching and training — whether local or distant, synchronous or asynchronous, using forms of teleconferencing, computer conferencing, the Internet, an intranet, and so on. We advise that you consult articles on the specific tech tools you have at your disposal — after you become comfortable in the basics of instruction.

Be Creative

Instructional media can be used in many ways in training and teaching. Here are just a few examples:

- An oceanographer took a high-powered microscope and video camera to the Gulf of Mexico in order to film organisms in their environment. She played her videotapes while teaching about those organisms.

- An instructor conducting training on workplace bias used pictures of people and asked the learners to guess the profession of each in order to show the effects of stereotypes.

- A soil and crop scientist used 2 x 2 color slides made from photographs of various grains so he could project pictures of the grains in a seminar.

- An expert in construction arranged for a live telephone conversation with another construction specialist.

- A speech therapist used tapes of old radio programs to highlight communication skills that enable listeners to conjure up images of scenes created for radio broadcast.

- An instructor used a video clip of a role-play situation to cause the learners to react and to generate discussion about what happened during that situation.

- An instructor conducting training on communication in the workplace distributed printed samples of flawed messages — e.g., e-mail, printed reports, and newsletters. The learners, with guidance from the instructor, discussed how each communication could be improved, which engaged them at the cognitive levels of analysis, synthesis, and evaluation.

- Some trainers use a flip chart as a checklist. The instructor starts the course by asking the learners to identify the things they hope to learn and/or questions they hope will be answered in the session. The instructor lists these on the flip chart. At the end of the session, the instructor reviews the items one by one, asking what the learners now know about it. If an item was not addressed or at least not fully, the instructor addresses it, promises to address it in a later session, or recommends sources where the learners can get information on it.

- A flip chart is often used as a *parking lot,* a place where the instructor jots any question or topic that would be a tangent from the session plan at that point. In this way the instructor can keep the class from getting off track. He or she then returns to the parked items later in the session or announces that they will be held for another session.

EVALUATE

Evaluate the Learners

In some instructional situations, generally in academic settings, the instructor evaluates the learners. If you do this, evaluate periodically, if possible, not just at the end of the course, and do it according to the behavioral objectives you set.

If — to take the example we used in the section on setting behavioral objectives — you set as an objective "On an asphalt track, the individual will run the 100-meter dash in less than 17 seconds," then that individual should go out to that asphalt track and run the 100-meter dash in less than 17 seconds.

If you specified performance levels — e.g., "in less than 15 seconds for an A, in less than 16 seconds for a B, in less than 17 seconds for a C, and in less than 18 seconds for a D," then the time would determine the grade for that objective.

If you're using paper-and-pencil tests, use various formats, not just true-and-false, not just multiple-choice, not just fill-in-the-blank, not just essay. Above all, don't use any means just because it's easiest for you.

Have the Learners Evaluate
the Course and You

If you want to be more effective in any future instructional responsibilities, it makes sense to have the learners of the course evaluate it and you.

In academic settings, there's often a form that instructors must use and rules to follow. Find out what is required of you and then do it. Following the policy and getting good ratings may be the two most important factors if you want to teach courses at that institution in the future.

In business settings, evaluations often consist of getting the reactions of the learners by asking questions such as the following:

- How useful was this course for you?

- How relevant to your job was the material covered?

- How well do you feel the instructor covered the material?

- How much did you enjoy the course?

This means of evaluating a course is popular primarily because it's quick and very easy to use and inexpensive to analyze.

This level of evaluation, however, is only one of the four levels in the model most widely used by professional trainers, the model proposed by Donald Kirkpatrick in 1994, which measures:

- reaction of learners — what they thought and felt about the course

- learning — how much they learned from the course

- behavior (transfer) — how much they apply what they've learned, how much their job performance improves

- results — how much the organization benefits from what the learners have learned from the course

You probably won't be able to evaluate your learners in terms of their behavior on the job and the results for the organization, but you should consider asking questions that will reveal what they've learned, not just how they feel about the course.

We recommend developing an evaluation form along the lines of the following.

Course Evaluation Form

How would you rate the instructor and/or course for each of the following statements?

Put an **X** following the descriptor that best describes how you feel about each statement.

1. The instructor demonstrated knowledge and expertise in the subject matter presented during the course.

   strongly agree ___   agree ___   neither agree nor disagree ___
                 disagree ___   strongly disagree ___

2. The instructor provided opportunities for us to engage in intellectual discussion.

   strongly agree ___   agree ___   neither agree nor disagree ___
                 disagree ___   strongly disagree ___

3. The course was relevant.

   strongly agree ___   agree ___   neither agree nor disagree ___
                 disagree ___   strongly disagree ___

4. The instructor allowed enough time for discussion.

   strongly agree ___   agree ___   neither agree nor disagree ___
                 disagree ___   strongly disagree ___

5. The instructor was positive and supportive throughout the program, and he/she encouraged participation.

   strongly agree ___   agree ___   neither agree nor disagree ___
                 disagree ___   strongly disagree ___

6. We achieved the objectives for the course.

   strongly agree ___   agree ___   neither agree nor disagree ___
                 disagree ___   strongly disagree ___

Add any comments. Feel free to explain your reaction to any of the items above.

KEEP CURRENT

If you expect to have instructional responsibilities in the future, remain knowledgeable about the subject matter. Read the journals in your field. Take notes, paying particular attention to new ideas and new research information. If you find a particularly good graphic, jot down the names of the author(s) and the publisher so you're ready to ask for permission to use the material if it's appropriate in a future course. Develop an appropriate system for storing your notes and related materials, so that you can easily retrieve those items when you need them.

Keep Your Materials Current and Effective

A logical corollary to keeping current is keeping your materials current. When your subject matter expertise changes, you should naturally update your materials.

But you should also attend to making your materials more effective if you do a course again. In addition to adding new information and possibly discarding old information, you should make changes according to your course evaluations, evaluations from the learners, and the notes you took immediately after every session.

You may want to start from zero. Reconsider your behavioral objectives. Are they really the most appropriate for what you expect course learners to know, understand, and/or be able to do at the end? Then, after you've made any changes in your objectives, think about whether you should be changing the map you followed in your schedule.

It's especially important to improve presentations. Review and revise your notes for each presentation, based on how effectively that presentation worked. Determine whether each of the materials you used is the best you could use in your instructional context.

Keep Fresh and Enthusiastic

Every course you conduct is something new to the learners. For you it can be something familiar and, with time, even old. But you should never feel old, because every time you conduct a course, it's different because of the learners. If you are attentive to their reactions, you can appreciate your course differently through their perspectives.

Helping people learn can be exciting, a way to expand your subject matter expertise and feel a greater sense of fulfillment. We wish you the best in your teaching and training activities!

TO LEARN MORE ABOUT ....

More about Setting Behavioral Objectives

Don Clark, "A Quick Guide to Writing Learning Objectives," The Training and Development Free Resource Center, http://www. Nwlink.com/~donclark/hrd/templates/objective tool.html, accessed Feb. 10, 2009.

More about the Hierarchy of Thinking

"Suggested Instructional Strategies for Use with Each Level of Bloom's Taxonomy," *ftp://ftp-fc.sc.egov.usda.gov/NEDC/isd/taxonomy.pdf*, accessed Feb. 10, 2009.

Richard C. Overbaugh and Lynn Schultz, "Bloom's Taxonomy," *http://www.odu.edu/educ/roverbau/Bloom/blooms_taxonomy.htm*, accessed Feb. 10, 2009.

Don Clark, "Learning Domains or Bloom's Taxonomy: Cognitive Domain," *http://www.nwlink.com/~Donclark/hrd/bloom.html*, accessed Feb. 10, 2009.

ABOUT THE AUTHORS

GLENN ROSS JOHNSON is a Professor Emeritus who served in various positions at Texas A&M University, where he worked for 30 years. Earlier in his career, he served as a teacher, reading consultant, assistant principal, and principal in public schools in Euclid, Ohio, and Clayton, Missouri. He has a BS in Education from Kent State University, an MA in Education from Ohio State University, and an EdD from Columbia University Teachers College.

Johnson's more than 50 publications have focused primarily on instructional strategies, including *First Steps to Excellence in College Teaching* (Atwood Publishing, CD Edition).

After serving as Professor and Head of the Department of Educational Curriculum and Instruction, Johnson, at the request of the President and Vice President of Texas A&M University, established and directed The Center for Teaching Excellence. The Center provided publications, seminars, workshops, and services to faculty members and teaching assistants.

While at Texas A&M University, Johnson developed a College Teaching Program that enabled adults holding bachelor's degrees and master's degrees in such fields as English, mathematics, physics, biology, business, and allied health to pursue a PhD in Educational Curriculum and Instruction. The program offered courses dealing with college teaching and curriculum, student personnel services, issues in higher education, and administration. Almost all of the students completing the program pursued dissertation research involving teaching in their subject area. Some of the graduates became college and university department chairs, associate deans, deans, and presidents.

ROBERT MAGNAN began writing and editing books in higher education after teaching for 13 years at three universities. He holds a BA in English and an MA in French from Michigan State University and a PhD in French from Indiana University.

Bob was Managing Editor of *The Teaching Professor* newsletter for seven years. He is the author of *147 Tips for Teaching Professors* (published also in Spanish and French) and *147 Practical Tips for Using Icebreakers with College Students* and the co-author of *Mentor in a Manual: Climbing the Academic Ladder to Tenure* (with A. Clay Schoenfeld). He has also edited some two dozen books in higher education, including *First Steps to Excellence in College Teaching* (Glenn Ross Johnson) and, most recently, *147 Practical Tips for Teaching Diversity* (William M. Timpson, Raymond Yang, Evelinn A. Borrayo, and Silvia Sara Canetto) and *Approaches to Communication: Trends in Global Communication Studies* (Susan Petrilli, editor).

Beyond higher education, Bob has written eight books and 10 condensed versions of books, edited more than 150 books, and translated and edited *Ordinary Hero* (*Le héros ordinaire*) by Yves Bertrand. He currently works as a freelance editor and author.

NOTES

NOTES